Graciously Broken

40 DAYS OF HOPE

AMANDA TORNBERG

www.thebluebirdpress.com

Gladewater, Texas

Graciously Broken: 40 Days of Hope
Copyright © 2021 by Amanda Tornberg
Cover design by Misty Sherman © 2021

Published by Bluebird Press, LLC, 15891 County Road 3110, Gladewater, TX 75647.

Bluebird Press presents this title in partnership with the author. The views expressed or implied in this work are those of the author. Bluebird Press provides our imprint seal representing design excellence, creative content, and high quality production.

All rights reserved. No part of this book may be used or reproduced in any manner whatsoever without written permission from the author except in the case of brief quotations embodied in critical articles and reviews.

Unless otherwise indicated, all Scripture quotations are from The ESV® Bible (The Holy Bible, English Standard Version®), copyright © 2001 by Crossway, a publishing ministry of Good News Publishers. Used by permission. All rights reserved.

Scripture quotations marked (NIV) are taken from the Holy Bible, New International Version®, NIV®. Copyright © 1973, 1978, 1984, 2011 by Biblica, Inc.™ Used by permission of Zondervan. All rights reserved worldwide. www.zondervan.com. The "NIV" and "New International Version" are trademarks registered in the United States Patent and Trademark Office by Biblica, Inc.™

Scripture quotations marked (NLT) are taken from the Holy Bible, New Living Translation, copyright ©1996, 2004, 2015 by Tyndale House Foundation. Used by permission of Tyndale House Publishers, Carol Stream, Illinois 60188. All rights reserved.

All italics, underlines, or parenthesis in quotations of Scripture have been added by the author.

Library of Congress Control Number: 2021901249

ISBN 978-0-9976856-2-6 (Paperback)
ISBN 978-0-9976856-3-3 (Epub)

To my God and Savior -
You have turned my mourning into dancing. You have removed my sackcloth and clothed me with joy so that my heart may sing your praises and not be silent. O my God,
I will give you praise forever.

And to my mom -
You're the one I have hurt the greatest but the one who has loved me through it all. Thank you for not giving up on me when it looked the most hopeless. I love you.

Table of Contents

Introduction	i
Darkness Disarmed	1
To Know by Experience	3
Chasing Shadows	5
Steadfast in Purpose	7
Safe Harbor	9
The Exchange of Glory	13
Crisis of Belief	17
Take a New Grip	19
Freedom Requires Diligence	21
Remain	23
Just Dust	25
But God	27
Commanding the Soul	29
Fix Your Face	31
Consider Jesus	33
But if Not	35
The Greatest Love	37
Love Expressed	41
Beauty in the Night	45
Not For Sale	49

Loving the Lie	51
Hiding Place	53
Awe and Wonder	55
Let Your Soul Sing	59
Awake, O Sleeper	61
Undeserved Kindness	63
A Life Exhausted	67
Compelling Grace	69
Yes and Amen	71
You Are Mine	73
Invitation to the Thirsty	75
Give Thanks	77
Like Those Who Dream	81
Intense but Measured	83
Carry Your Cross	87
Anchor for the Soul	91
The Purity of Conscience	93
What's Your End?	95
For the Joy	97
Fall Down	101
Endnotes	105
Bibliography	107
Order Information	111

Introduction

I would like to share with you a glimpse into my story. My story, I would imagine, is going to be similar to some of yours in ways, and maybe not so similar in other ways. I am the youngest of two children, and I was brought up in a home where church was a priority. We were at church every time the doors were open. I was taught right from wrong, what you're supposed to do and what you're not supposed to do. Unfortunately, and unintentionally, I was also taught to put on an appearance of perfection. My subconscious mantra was, "Don't ever let anyone know what's really going on. Play the part!" I did my best, but on the inside I felt like I was dying.

Like any good church kid, I knew the details of Jesus. I was taught that He died for me so I would not have to go to Hell, and since Hell was *not* where I wanted to end up, I would pray at almost every youth camp I ever attended in hopes that maybe this time my prayer for salvation would be enough. Like I said, I knew some basic details but had absolutely no idea what it all really meant.

My understanding of God, at the time, was that He expected me to live a certain way. I believed that His love was conditional and dependent upon whether I deserved it in any given moment or not. As a result, from a very young age I struggled with feeling broken, damaged, unlovable, and hopeless. I was certain that if anyone ever knew the truth about me, they would agree.

I remember having an almost constant overwhelming desperation to find something, some way, to be okay. I had feelings of emptiness in me that longed to be filled. The longings set me on a course that would become many years of searching endlessly to find something that might satisfy the ache, mend the brokenness, or bring some glimmer of hope. But as the years passed, the brokenness and despair only deepened, and any hope I had of ever feeling any better vanished.

I share this with you because I believe that although the circumstances of our lives may be different, we all share the same condition. You may not recognize it if you tend to feel as though you've got it all together, but I believe that is only because you have placed your attention and your affection on some lesser hope – a lesser hope such as the worldly hope of achievement for example. And in this case, you likely won't realize your condition until you are no longer able to achieve.

See, I believe we have this one thing in common: all of humanity experiences a deep longing for some sort of meaning and purpose. We all look for something to define our worth. And I believe this because all of our stories originated in the same way: "In the beginning, God . . ." (Gen. 1:1).

In order to understand the true nature of our condition, we must look back to where it all began. We see through the creation story that God's design was for Adam and Eve to have fellowship with Him, and for them to walk with Him in humility and submission in order to feel whole. But what we see through the events in Genesis that recount the fall of humanity is they wanted their own way. As a result of their rebellion and sin, the peace they had with God was lost, a void was left in its place, and ever since all of humanity has been on a frantic search to find what is missing.

This is all of our stories. We've all gone our own way. We all know something is missing, and we feel it deep down if we are brave enough to admit it. The problems come when we look to anything other than God to fill what is missing. And this world is not short on options. It offers us many false hopes like the thrill of money, high status, the praise of men, who we are married to, our children, or our right behavior. We try to pacify ourselves by taking comfort in food, in romantic fiction, in comparison, and in gossip.

We exhaust ourselves in a never-ending desperation for more of whatever it is we think will satisfy the longing and cover the shame. Yet, in all attempts we come up empty, and our thirst is never fully quenched.

Listen, in His compassion, our God has offered us a Better Hope! And He invites us to come find life in Him. Isaiah 55:1-3 extends to us an invitation:

> Come, all you who are thirsty, come to the waters . . . Why spend money on what is not bread (what doesn't fill you up), and your labor on what does not satisfy (what doesn't quench your thirst)? Listen, listen to me, and eat what is good, and you will delight in the richest of fare. Give ear and come to me; listen, that you may

live. I will make an everlasting covenant with you, my faithful love promised to David. (NIV, but words in parenthesis added by author for clarification)

All of our worldly hopes are deceptive. With each failed attempt the void deepens, and our frantic search continues. In Isaiah 55 above, we see the compassion of our God and His solution to our problem. He is pointing us to Jesus, the true Bread of Life and the true Living Water. Yes, Jesus - a new hope, and a better hope. In fact, just a couple chapters prior in Isaiah 53:1-6, which was written hundreds of years before Christ walked the earth, God began foretelling through the prophet how to identify the One who would be this new and better hope for us. This is what he envisioned from God:

> Who has believed what he has heard from us? And to whom has the arm of the Lord been revealed? . . . He was despised and rejected by men, a man of sorrows and acquainted with grief . . . he was despised, and we esteemed him not. Surely he has borne our griefs and carried our sorrows; yet we esteemed him stricken, smitten by God, and afflicted. But he was pierced for our transgressions; he was crushed for our iniquities; upon him was the chastisement that brought us peace, and with his wounds we are healed. All we like sheep have gone astray; we have turned - every one - to his own way; and the Lord has laid on him the iniquity of us all. (Isaiah 53:1, 3-6)

Listen, Jesus is what our God is inviting us to receive. Our God knows that our problem is not physical, but spiritual. Therefore, our solution is not circumstantial, but relational. Our God knows this, and so through Christ, He has made a better way!

My desire is not that you would walk away from this book thinking how you need to be better and do more. My prayer is that you walk away completely overcome by the love of God. My prayer is that your heart would be undone by the beauty of the undeserved grace of God that meets you in your brokenness. My prayer is that you would come to find the only One that can truly satisfy your emptiness. I'm glad you have chosen to join me on this 40-day journey.

DAY ONE

Darkness Disarmed

"Let us hold fast to the confession of our hope without wavering, for he who promised is faithful."
Hebrews 10:23

Do you ever feel what people sometimes call "a darkness of the soul?" The weight settles in like fog in a valley. You feel lost in obscurity like shadows in the night. In the night, all hope can seem lost. You can't quite see your way through the engulfing gloom, and you wonder if there is anything that can pierce through the palpable darkness.

Do not let yourself be dismayed. Take heart! Our Christ has come! He said, "I have come into the world as light, so that whoever believes in me may not remain in darkness" (Jn. 12:46).

Behold the Light! See what splendor, what brilliance! Hold securely to your faith by keeping His victory in mind. Listen, there is no shadow in His light. Light does not yield to darkness. It does not consent. It will not buckle.

Hold fast to the truth we find in John 1:5, "The light shines in the darkness, and the darkness has not overcome it."

Hear me, our struggles are not with what is seen. Our struggles are with the rulers, authorities, and powers that have already been ultimately disarmed and defeated by Christ! They know we struggle with doubting that, and so they play with our minds. Do you feel beaten? Do you feel overwhelmed? Do you feel like you've got nothing left to give? Look to the cross! "God made you alive in Christ. He forgave us all our sins, having canceled the charge . . . he took it away, nailing it to the cross. And having disarmed the powers and authorities, he made a public spectacle of them, triumphing over them by the cross" (Col. 2:13-15, NIV). Their accusations can no longer legally stand if we don't let them. And they certainly don't have the power to separate us from the love of Christ (Rom. 8:37-39).

The One who made us alive, the One who forgives, the One who took our sin and our shame by bearing them on the cross has triumphed over darkness and has given us victory through His resurrected life!

O disheartened one, let that truth cause your heart to burn. Our Jesus has disarmed your darkness!

Song of Worship: "Light of the World" by Lauren Daigle

DAY TWO

To Know by Experience

"Now you shall see what I will do ... and you shall know that I am the Lord Your God ..."
Exodus 6:1, 7

Let me set this up for you. God sent Moses to Egypt to deliver His people. When he got there, he performed the miraculous signs God had enabled him to do, and in response, the elders believed and worshiped the Lord. I can imagine their excitement as they anticipated their deliverance after years of harsh slavery! Their minds raced, "God has seen us! He has sent a deliverer! Surely this is it! Yes, Moses! Go! Go tell Pharaoh all that God has said!" So, Moses went and told Pharaoh that God said to let His people go. However, Pharaoh saw the Israelites in their state of slavery and decided it spoke to the weakness of their God, so he refused.

We often do the same thing. Here's what I mean. We look to our circumstances or the condition of others and allow those things to determine for us the character and the power of God. Pharaoh saw the slavery of the Israelites and felt there was no reason for him to be threatened by their God. If their God was so powerful then why were they enslaved in the first place? But listen, His character and power are not defined by our perceptions, circumstances, or opinions.

Pharaoh not only refused to set the Israelites free, he also put more work on them. As a result, they decided they no longer wanted God's deliverance. Their faith in God was eclipsed by their fear of Pharaoh. You see, that's what happens when we allow circumstances to determine God's love for us or determine His power to save us. We no longer want His deliverance and, instead, seek relief through the very things that have enslaved us.

At the end of Exodus 5, Moses asked the Lord why He would send him with a message of deliverance if He was only going to allow more problems for His people. And the Lord responded, "Now you will see . . ."

I believe God was telling Moses, "Look, I know what it looks like, but you're about to see who I am. I am not defined by your opinion of me. I'm going to bring you out, not because you deserve it or because Pharaoh allowed it. I'm going to do this because when I do, you are going to know by your own experience what it means for me to be your Lord.

Song of Worship: "Great Things" by Phil Wickham

DAY THREE

"I say this that no one may delude you with plausible arguments ... as you received Christ Jesus as the Lord, so walk in him, rooted and built up in him and established in the faith, just as you were taught, abounding in thanksgiving."
Colossians 2:4, 6-7

So often, we are lured away by our own error and foolishness. We put our hope in lesser things and when they fail us, we come up empty. We get angry with God, and we feel like He has failed us in some way. Instead of taking our disappointments to God, we turn to others who will tell us what we want to hear. Doing this puts us in great peril. The reason I say that is because none of us normally need intense moments of temptation in order to sin. We just need to be able to justify it in some way or another. Others are far too often ready to help us do that.

In our recklessness we allow lust, conformity, indifference, compromise, and even religion to bring us to ruin. We begin to set the wisdom of the world up above the wisdom of God. We coddle ourselves with the part of the gospel that says Christ forgives sin, while we ignore the other part of the gospel that calls us to die to ourselves and live in Him.

The way to combat this self-deception is to walk in the way of the One we have professed to believe. We are saved by grace through faith, and that is exactly how we must walk - by grace through faith. Stop chasing good feelings. Too often we want our emotions stirred but want our toes left untrampled.

We must be careful not to be drawn away from Christ, back into the shadows of our former lives. Our self-centered efforts to control our own passions, do not achieve for us a life of righteousness. A life of true righteousness only comes as we set our affections on Christ.

Listen, the fulfillment you seek is found in an intimate, growing relationship with Christ, not the trappings of this world or in how good you believe yourself to be as a person. We must root ourselves in His love for us, not in our love for Him since that gives us the praise. The love of God has been revealed through the person and work of Christ, and we must allow Him to be the spring by which our faith flows.

We, in gratitude, set our affections on Christ. He is our only hope for change. May we be daily overwhelmed and fall more and more in love with the One who loved us first.

Song of Worship: "Never Going Back" by United Pursuit

DAY FOUR

Steadfast in Purpose

"... remain faithful to the Lord with steadfast purpose."
Acts 11:23

The context behind this passage was that the believers of the early church had been scattered because of persecution. It was a persecution that had only recently resulted in the death of one of their own, named Stephen. Stephen was the first official Christian martyr, and the persecutors certainly intended that by killing him for his faith, it would end the spread of the gospel. However, what we see is that it actually fanned the gospel into flame throughout the land.

How? For many of us, it is difficult to fathom because we are consumed with our own comfort and safety. Thoughts take priority in our minds such as, "What will people think of me? And will I lose my friends if I share with them about God?" For the early church, however, they may have fled from the persecution for safety reasons, but they did not abandon their purpose. They did not let the opinion of man or fear of consequences keep them from making known the work of the Lord on behalf of sinners. They knew from what depths they had been saved, and they didn't want anyone to miss the salvation that was available to them if they would only believe. They took to heart the warning we see in Romans 10:14, "How then will they call on him in whom they have not believed? And how are they to believe in him whom they have never heard? And how are they to hear without someone preaching?" They didn't allow their own suffering to cause resentment in their hearts toward God or cause them to turn aside from their purpose.

Do you ever experience seasons in life where it feels like the harassment of the enemy will never end? Maybe you are experiencing a time of great suffering and you are wondering the point of it all. Or, perhaps, you are just allowing everyday irritations to steel your focus. Let your heart be encouraged with this truth: God does see you and He is not indifferent. Like Joseph, we can declare with firm assurance that although the enemy's intention is for evil, God is working it out for good and for the glory of His great name (Gen. 50:20)!

O fellow believer, "be strong in the Lord and in the strength of his might" (Eph. 6:10). When you feel you have nothing left, remain steadfast.

Song of Worship: "See A Victory" by Elevation Worship

DAY FIVE

Safe Harbor

"... do not be anxious about anything, but in everything by prayer and supplication with thanksgiving let your requests be made known to God. And the peace of God, which surpasses all understanding, will guard your hearts and your minds in Christ Jesus."
Philippians 4:6-7

I believe some of the worst advice I hear people give is "follow your heart." Scripture tells us in Jeremiah 17:9 that our heart is "deceitful above all things, and desperately sick." We shouldn't follow it. In Proverbs 4:23 we are told to guard our hearts, and for good reason since our hearts can so easily determine our course. Luke 6:45 tells us that "out of the abundance of the heart his mouth speaks." A heart that is not renewed from its corruption by Christ and daily maintained in Christ, has a huge risk of leading toward error and corrupt paths. So we must constantly guard it for holiness.

According to The NAS New Testament Greek Lexicon, the

heart (*kardia*) refers to the seat of the desires, feelings, affections, and passions.[1] We are told in 2 Corinthians 5:17, that in Christ we are new creatures, the old is gone and the new has come. So listen, as believers we are given a new heart and a new nature, but we also see in the book of Romans that this new nature we have been given is at war with the old nature within us.

Why am I saying all of this? Because although we have been given a new nature and are no longer slaves to sin, our desires, feelings, affections, and passions can still, at times, long for those old things. That's why I believe we need to be careful with the advice to "follow your heart." I think the better advice is to be careful to guard your heart, evaluate it, and ask God to change that which is still at war with His life in us.

Our natural heart tells us that we will find protection in our anger, in our isolation, in our perfectionism, and the list could continue. It's our hearts that deceive us into thinking that we have given God rightful authority in our lives when, in reality, it's possibly our addictions, bitterness, doubts, greed, lust, and self-pity that make our decisions and give us orders. We sing praises to our God with our mouths while our hearts are worshipping our jobs, kids, money, relationships, and even our ministries.

In His love, we find a safe place to acknowledge that there are things flowing in our hearts that could threaten everything. There are lies we are believing, and maybe even secret sins with which we are toying.

Hear me, His love is our safe harbor. Therefore, "let us then with confidence draw near to the throne of grace, that we may receive mercy and find grace to help in time of need" (Heb. 4:16).

Song of Worship: "Jesus is Better" by Austin Stone Worship

DAY SIX

The Exchange of Glory

"For although they knew God, they did not honor him as God or give thanks to him, but they became futile in their thinking, and their foolish hearts were darkened. Claiming to be wise, they became fools, and exchanged the glory of the immortal God for images resembling mortal man and birds and animals and creeping things. Therefore, God gave them up in the lusts of their hearts to impurity, to the dishonoring of their bodies among themselves, because they exchanged the truth about God for a lie and worshipped and served the creature rather than the Creator..."
Romans 1:21-25

"They exchanged the truth . . . for a lie" - Don't miss this. That's where they ended up, not where they started. We've all been there, right? We've all been there wondering how we ended up where we are now. It starts for us as it did with them, with a lack of esteem for God. Think of the Israelites. They had certainly experienced God's presence in their lives and His saving mercy towards them. They had witnessed God miraculously deliver them from slavery and then continue to perform one miracle after another as He led them through the desert. Yet instead of thanking Him, they were unsatisfied with His provision and continually complained and grumbled. Then they began to lust after the things the world could offer. I'm sure it started small. It was probably hardly noticeable at first, like a thought entertained too long. Or maybe it started with a small justification like, "I'll just take one look. It's not that bad. One look won't hurt anyone." Or possibly it was an attitude left unchecked, like an unacknowledged hurt or a letdown that eventually led to resentment and bitterness. Maybe they filled in the following blanks in their own way and decided to turn from God rather than trust Him.

God why didn't you _____?

How could you _____?

If You loved us, You would have _____.

If You were good, You wouldn't have _____.

As a result of focusing on thoughts and feelings like these, maybe the lies began to carry more weight in their hearts than His beauty. Their thinking became pointless, and they became reckless with their hearts. And then, finally, God gave them over to themselves. He let them have what they thought they wanted. What a chilling warning this is to us.

I find myself wondering how much pain and heartache could be avoided if we would simply be willing to ask ourselves some questions along the way. We should be willing to ask ourselves questions like these: "Is this thought based on truth? Is what I am about to turn to *really* what I ultimately want? Were my past mistakes and consequences really so good that I want to repeat them again?" Take time to ask yourself these questions when you feel yourself spiraling.

Assess your current state today by asking yourself:
What is carrying ultimate weight in my heart, truth or lies? Am I asking God to reveal the truth to me? Or am I leaning on my own understanding?

Song of Worship: "Nothing I Hold Onto" by Will Reagan & United Pursuit

DAY SEVEN

Crisis of Belief

"God is our refuge and strength, a very present help in trouble. Therefore we will not fear though the earth gives way, though the mountains be moved into the heart of the sea, though its waters roar and foam, though the mountains tremble at its swelling…"
Psalm 46:1-3

We all have come, or will come, to places in our lives where we are faced with a crisis of belief. These occasions are times when we must choose whether we are going to believe God or not. We must put what we profess to believe into action. It's easy to say that you believe God is good, that He is faithful, and that He is loving, but when your world begins to give way, what do your actions reveal that you truly believe about God? Often in these times we tend to try and take back control of our lives because we feel that He's not doing a good enough job. We turn to some other means for rescue or relief because we feel it's just too risky trusting Him to lead us.

I love how in this passage the psalmist reminds us of who God is and uses God's character as the basis for what he was going to say next. Basically, he's saying, "God is our refuge and our strength. And this God is not just any god, but *The* God! He is the One who put the planets into motion and told the sea how far it could go. *That's* our God. He is always there to assist us in our troubles. And because that is who He is, we don't have to fear, no matter the circumstances. Though disaster strikes, He is all powerful, and He is with us. He is our safe haven, our security, our support. He is a true help, a real help, a complete help."

Listen, that's why we don't have to fear when calamity strikes. If you are doubting and struggling in your faith today, my prayer is that you would hold fast to His character and turn to Him to find your support. These storms you are facing will not sweep over you, for you are not facing them alone. When the tempests obscure your vision of Him, remember that He has promised to be with you. And He who has promised is faithful!

Song of Worship: "The Rock Won't Move" by
Vertical Worship

DAY EIGHT

"... the Lord stood by him and said, 'Take courage, for as you have testified to the facts about me in Jerusalem, so you must testify also in Rome.'"
Acts 23:11

Whenever I picture Paul, I usually picture this strong, fearless, never-a-doubt-in-his-mind kind of guy. Realistically, though, he was only a man. No doubt, he had questions just as we do at times. And I know he must have experienced overwhelming emotions, like the kind of emotions that come from fear and doubt that unsettle our hearts and minds, or maybe the kind of emotions that wage war against a human's resolve. Paul was a person that struggled just like you and me.

But oh, how very present a Savior we have! For He came and stood by him and spoke to him. He reassured him in his time of distress, not only with His presence, but by reminding him of the bigger picture.

The Savior does the same for us. We are told in Psalm 34:18-

19 that, "The Lord is near to the brokenhearted and saves the crushed in spirit. Many are the afflictions of the righteous, but the Lord delivers him out of them all."

This life is full of difficulties. At times the burdens seem more than we can bear. We become weary of the battle. We feel defeated and overwhelmed by the fear of the unknown. Our courage starts to wane, and all resolve seems to vanish.

In those moments we must remember that our God is still near. He's still in control, and there's a bigger picture in play. Because we know this to be true, we can heed the exhortation given to us by the author of Hebrews, "So take a new grip with your tired hands and strengthen your weak knees. Mark out a straight path for your feet *so that* those who are weak and lame will not fall but become strong" (Heb. 12:12-13, NLT, italics added for emphasis).

Listen, in the midst of opposition, be strengthened in resolve. When uncertainty causes anxiety, stand full of all assurance that our God is doing something! We can't always see it, but we can still know it.

Song of Worship: "If You Want Me To" by Ginny Owens

DAY NINE

Freedom Requires Diligence

"For freedom Christ has set us free; stand firm therefore, and do not submit again to a yoke of slavery."
Galatians 5:1

It's so easy to become forgetful of our former slavery. So readily we yield to yet another form of bondage and forfeit the very freedom we once treasured. We are tempted to compare the current manifestation of our brokenness to the former. What I mean is when we look back in our personal history and remember our worst sins or our sins with very devastating effects, we are often tempted to view what we consider smaller levels of sin as harmless or "not that bad" when compared to our past. When we do this, it blinds us to sin's danger and conversely enslaves us anew. No amount of sin is harmless.

Galatians 5:7 asks this truth: "You were running well. Who hindered you from obeying the truth?"

So many things can creep in and hinder our obedience to

truth. We allow comparison to kill our contentment and then when we feel unsatisfied, we begin turning back to old appetites hoping that, maybe this time, they will deliver on their promises. However, they never do, and we are left even more empty and discontented. Our enemy is so quick to try and hinder our pursuit of holiness. He is very adept at telling half-truths and causing us to doubt the goodness of our God. He tries to convince us that our God is holding out on us, or that He just doesn't want us to be happy. Pretty soon, there we go again being dominated by mistrust and accusations.

We are all vulnerable to such entrapments. Has something cut in on you and gotten in your way? What have you allowed to get you off course? Listen, we must be diligent with our thoughts. Scripture encourages us to take every thought captive. We are to be ready to destroy any argument or opinion that sets itself up against the knowledge of God (2 Cor. 10:5). Thoughts left unchecked lead to overwhelming feelings, and those negative emotions will almost always lead to detrimental behaviors.

Don't be careless with your faith. He has set you free so that you would be free. Stand firm then and remember, continual freedom from the entanglements of this world requires your diligence.

Song of Worship: "Running In Circles" by United Pursuit

DAY TEN

"But the unbelieving Jews stirred up the Gentiles and poisoned their minds against the brothers. <u>So</u> they remained for a long time, speaking boldly for the Lord, who bore witness to the word of his grace ..."
Acts 14:2-3

"So" - One small word makes all the difference sometimes. It would make more sense if it said, "but they remained." However, it states, "<u>So</u> they remained." They didn't remain "in spite of" but "because of."

As I read this, I thought of 2 Corinthians 5:14, "For the love of Christ controls us, because we have concluded this: that one has died for all, therefore, all have died; and he died for all, that those who live might no longer live for themselves but for him who for their sake died and was raised."

I believe this verse reveals their motivation for staying. Paul and Barnabas stayed because they were compelled by love, rather than by fear or pride. They understood they were saved for a purpose and it wasn't so they could be safe and comfortable. They knew the truth they were sharing was salvation for those who would believe, and they would rather stay and risk everything than have the Gentiles miss out on the grace being offered to them. See, for Paul and Barnabas, it was the love they received from Christ that compelled them to remain.

Oh that we, too, might remain steadfast in the midst of slander. It's so easy when others rise up against us to either respond the same way or flee to avoid all drama. When we react in one of those ways, they see nothing different about us and the work of the Lord is hindered. I pray that, today, you would allow love to control your reaction. Rather than having the attitude that you will invest in others, "in spite of" their brokenness, I pray your heart would be moved to be a witness to them "because of" their brokenness and "because of" their need for the grace and love of Christ.

Remain purposely, my friend, and speak boldly for the Lord. Speak bodly in action as much as with words, so that others might see evidence of His grace in you and, thereby, receive it one day for themselves.

Song of Worship: "Spirit Lead me" by Influence Music & Michael Ketterer

DAY ELEVEN

"As a father shows compassion to his children, so the Lord shows compassion to those who fear him. For he knows our frame; he remembers that we are dust."
Psalm 103:13-14

Have you ever struggled to believe that God is for you and not against you? I love the scripture above for that reason. Time and time again, the Holy Spirit has used this passage to impart to me hope amidst my failures. I would strive to be so faithful and when I failed, I would spiral into a pit of despair thinking, "How could I love God and do this? I must be such a disappointment to Him;" or "I'm sure He's sick of me now. This time I've gone too far." On and on the lies would rush in, bringing with them a dark hopelessness.

That's when the enemy would begin whispering old familiar lies like, "You'll never be anything more than you always were. It's only a matter of time before you are right back to living like you were before Christ." The longer I allowed those lies to take reign in my heart, the harder it became to distinguish the truth. I was once again believing God's love for me hinged on my own "goodness." Buying into that lie can be so damaging to our Christian walk and witness.

The truth is, God doesn't expect us to be perfect. He will not forsake us in our weaknesses. He simply wants us to bring our failures to Him so that we can be reminded of who He is and, thereby, find the grace we need to stand once again. Don't be afraid. Don't allow your feelings of disappointment about yourself keep you from running into the arms of your loving heavenly Father. He is kind. He is able to sympathize with our weaknesses, and He takes into consideration our frame.

Today, I pray that you would allow your heart to be stirred into confidence as you remember that our God knows how He has formed you to need Him. He remembers that you are mere dust, constantly in need of grace.

Song of Worship: "Beautiful Things" by Gungor

DAY TWELVE

"And you were dead in the trespasses and sins in which you once walked ... and were by nature children of wrath ... But God, being rich in mercy, because of the great love with which he loved us, even when we were dead in our trespasses, made us alive together with Christ ..."
Ephesians 2:1-5

"But God"- Two words that are at the heart of the gospel. It's such a small phrase that carries with it an amazing message.

Jon Bloom says it this way, "'But God.' These two words are overflowing with gospel. For sinners like you and me who were lost and completely unable to save ourselves from our dead-set rebellion against God, there may not be two more hopeful words that we could utter."[1]

All of us experience times of wanting to give up, times when nothing seems to go right, times when everything seems stacked against us, and times when we feel we have gone too far or have done too much. Far too often, all we see is our failures and forget to hold fast to the truths that could come after the "But God."

Yes, there was a time I was living in disobedience, gratifying every single lust of my flesh. It was a time when I was separated from God, without any hope. I was dead in my sin and deserving destruction ". . .but God!" Even though I was dead in my sin, He came to me and offered me life in Christ! When all else failed, there was still a "but God!" He is rich in mercy - loaded with mercy - and boundless in love, no matter the offense!

Listen, dear one, God's love for you is abundant, and His mercy is never-ending, so you are never beyond hope or another "but God." Grab hold of that truth because it gives you a position from which to fight. It's one small perspective-shift that can change everything!

Listen to what the late James Montgomery Boice said about it: "May I put it quite simply? If you understand those two words - 'But God' - they will save your soul. If you recall them daily and live by them, they will transform your life completely."

Song of Worship: "Simple Gospel" by United Pursuit

DAY THIRTEEN

Commanding the Soul

"I wait for the Lord, my soul waits, and in his word I hope; my soul waits for the Lord more than watchmen for the morning, more than watchmen for the morning."
Psalm 130:5-6

Have you ever experienced sleepless nights? I'm talking about the kind of nights where you are lying in wait with only your own thoughts to keep you company, nights where the anxieties of life are bearing down on your faith. In moments like these, it seems as though morning will never come.

We have similar experiences within our souls. We experience these sleepless nights of the soul during the times when it seems as though we have been left alone to fight the war that wages within our hearts and minds, when it appears that God is nowhere in sight, or when our fears are screaming at us and our diffilcut circumstances eclipse God's affections toward us. We pray, but our prayers seem to be met with indifference.

This is not a strange event. Since the beginning of time,

those who have hoped in God have experienced times just like these, and during such periods they, too, have undergone spiritual anxiety and emotional struggle. R.C. Sproul refers to times like these as "the dark night of the soul." So, the question is: What is to be our response during these "dark nights?"

I believe we see the answer to this question, not only in our scripture for the day, but also in Psalm 42:5: "Why are you cast down, O my soul, and why are you in turmoil within me? Hope in God; for I shall again praise him, my salvation and my God."

I absolutely love how in this verse the Psalmist is commanding His soul. When I read this, it comes across as though he is almost reprimanding his soul by saying "Why are you so downcast? Why are you so unsettled in spirit? Hope in God!"

Listen, our feelings are going to come and go. Troubles will come and go. Doubts will invade. But they can all be forced out when we remind our souls of the truth. We declare to ourselves and preach to ourselves that although we may not see the deliverance, we will choose to believe the Word of our Lord. As sure as I am that the sun will rise, so sure am I that my God will act on your behalf! He is not indifferent to our suffering. Expect either growth or relief! Believe it! It will come! Listen - though it lingers - wait!

Song of Worship: "You'll Come" by Hillsong UNITED

DAY FOURTEEN

"But the Lord God helps me; therefore I have not been disgraced; therefore I have set my face like a flint, and I know that I shall not be put to shame."
Isaiah 50:7

My God loves me. He's so good to me. I can honestly say I believe that to be more true than I believe anything else. The problem is I don't always saturate myself in that truth. I don't always allow the reality of it to sink deep down, in the midst of circumstances.

I consider myself a very alert driver (although others may not agree), but I will admit that I have a tendency to take my eyes off the road when something else gets my attention. This is a problem since I tend to go in whatever direction my eyes are looking. A distraction will even occasionally cause me to veer toward oncoming traffic or a ditch. I have learned this illustration is very similar to my struggle with temptation. I tend to head in the direction of the attention of the eyes of my heart.

I love my God, but if I'm honest there are times that my actions reflect that I'm loving something else more. Something else gets my attention, and when that happens, I am apt to get entangled in sin. I hate this tendency in me and have spent a lot of time agonizing over it. I can give you all sorts of reasons why I'm susceptible to certain sins, but none of those explanations justify me to give into them.

In moments when the grip of sin seems to be clutched so tightly around me, the Holy Spirit reminds me of today's scripture. It's His hand offering a way out of the grasp of sin. And then I know what I must do. I must set my face like stone and be determined to do the will of my God. I must trust that His Spirit will give me every grace needed to stand faithful. Listen, believer, if we want change in our lives, we must continually command the eyes of our hearts to fix their gaze on Christ.

Charles Spurgeon once said, "My great object is to lead you to love him who so loved you that he set his face like a flint in his determination to save you. O ye redeemed ones, on whose behalf this strong resolve was made - ye who have been bought by the precious blood of the steadfast, resolute Redeemer - come and think awhile of him, that your hearts may burn within you, and that your faces may be set like flints to live and die for him who lived and died for you."[1] Take a minute to get your gaze fixed on Christ today.

Song of Worship: "Grace to Grace" by Hillsong Worship

DAY FIFTEEN

Consider Jesus

"Consider him who endured from sinners such hostility against himself, so that you may not grow weary and fainthearted."
Hebrews 12:3

With all the turmoil in this world it is vital that our eyes remain fixed on the right thing. If not, worry and anxiety over life's circumstances will cause us to look to ourselves to manipulate for control. Fears will begin to crowd out our faith and our security will be shaken. We must be careful not to allow life's circumstances to form an opinion of God for us that seeks to undermine our faith. See, we tend to think our circumstances determine the character of our God. But in reality, it is the character of our God that is to influence our view of circumstances.

So, we fix our eyes on Jesus and consider Him. I love how in chapter 11 of Hebrews the author lists the great believers of old who were commended for their faith. They refused to allow their circumstances to determine their truth. All of them looked forward to what was promised, walked out into the unknown, and believed the unfathomable. They gave up their riches and their places of prominence, and in so doing, they offered to the Lord the best of what they had. Scripture tells us that they all died in faith, not having received the things promised, but only having seen them and greeted them from afar. They were able to do this because they knew this world was not their home, and that meant they were strangers here on earth who were just passing through. We are told that some of them conquered kingdoms while others were tortured, mocked, flogged, put in chains, and imprisoned. Some were even stoned, sawn in two, and killed with the sword. All of them, however, endured until the end because they knew in whom they had believed, and they considered Him who had made the promise to be faithful.

Like the heroes of faith, we too, will be called into the unknown. We may be asked to exchange riches and prominence in order to follow Christ. We will endure suffering, and some might even have to give their lives. No matter what you are facing today, consider Jesus! Know that you, too, can trust in whom you have believed.

Song of Worship: "Take a Moment" by Will Reagan & United Pursuit

DAY SIXTEEN

"If this be so, our God whom we serve is able to deliver us from the burning fiery furnace, and he will deliver us out of your hand, O king. But if not, be it known to you, O king, that we will not serve your gods or worship the golden image you have set up."
Daniel 3:17-18

All too often we allow the culture around us to determine what's morally right and wrong. Our standard for holiness depends on who is standing next to us. It's tempting in today's society to compromise our beliefs, because if we don't, we are called intolerant.

The biblical account of Shadrach, Meshach, and Abednego challenged such apathy and lukewarmness. They were living in a culture full of idolatry, not unlike our own, yet they stood against the accepted norm. The king issued a proclamation that all men should worship the idol he had raised, and if anyone refused, they would be put to death. The king wasn't restricting them from worshipping any other god they chose, they just had to bow down to his idol in addition to their own.

We run a great risk when we begin to forfeit our belief in the truth of Scripture for the sake of "tolerance" and "unity." Gregg T. Johnson communicates the danger in this when he says, "While the idea of 'unity' may seem noble, the way it is achieved may not be. Often, it requires compromising - if not entirely abandoning essential principles of faith in order that we may 'get together.'"[1]

What you see in the testimony of these three men is they would rather suffer than be disloyal to their God. They didn't have to think about it. They knew where they stood. For them, it was better to worship the one true God through death, than live a life of insult toward Him.

They were comforted by their belief that God was fully capable of rescuing them. For them, it wasn't a matter if He *would*. Their comfort and confidence came because they were convinced He *could*. This fact alone reminded them God was entirely in control and would have it play out just how it needed to for the bigger eternal plan, and these men were willing to be used in whatever way necessary to accomplish His purposes. Where in your life are you compromising in the name of "tolerance?" Hear me, this isn't about the sin in anyone else's life. Insult, condemnation, or fits of rage don't motivate others to worship our King - love does. We can stand in truth and still love. They go together.

Song of Worship: "Burn Us Up" by Shane & Shane

DAY SEVENTEEN

The Greatest Love

"Greater love has no one than this, that someone lay down his life for his friends."
John 15:13

Sadly, so many of us have misunderstood the heart of God. As a result, we have sometimes dismissed the very love for which we are so desperate. For some of us, our misunderstanding of the heart of God originated from painful experiences involving people who have professed to know His love. For others of us, our misunderstanding of the heart of God originated when our desire for immediate self-gratification was not met by God too many times and we began to believe He didn't care. No matter the circumstance that brought it about, the result is the same. We bought into the lie that our situation is verification of His love or lack of love for us. When a thought that God might not love us is left unchecked, eventually we spiral further down into thinking He is disappointed or angry with us, and we slowly begin walking in condemnation instead of in His love and grace.

However, Scripture reveals He didn't draw us in just so He could condemn us. John 3:17 says, "For God did not send his Son into the world to condemn the world, but in order that the world might be saved through him." And in our verse for the day we see it was Christ's great love that went to such lengths to save us: "Greater love has no one than this, that someone lay down his life for his friends" (Jn. 15:13). Believe me, no one has laid down their life for you like Christ did. No one has given up what God gave up to become a limited man, and then laid down that life in total humility to save you and me. Greater love has no one seen! It was the only way to save us, and He did it because of His deep love. Love is who He is, and He could not deny Himself by not extending to us the way to salvation.

Oh, cherished one, you are adored by the only One who matters. There is no greater evidence that can be offered than what He has already done. His love for you moved Him to action on your behalf. Romans 5:8 says it beautifully, ". . . but God shows his love for us in that while we were still sinners, Christ died for us." In the midst of our sin and at our very worst when we despised Him, rejected Him, and spit in His face, He gave up His life so we might find life in Him.

The good news of Christ is the beautiful truth of such great love and power that we are never the same once we have encountered it. The gospel changes everything! Many of us have heard it so many times. We have a head knowledge, but we've never let ourselves believe it with our hearts. We have been always learning but never acknowledging the truth for ourselves. We have accumulated knowledge, but never let it direct our lives. We've never let it in enough to be brought to our knees by it, or let it sink in enough to be in awe of it. Open your heart and let the truth in today.

Song of Worship: "Love Like This" by Lauren Daigle

DAY EIGHTEEN

"A new command I give to you, that you love one another:
just as I have loved you, you also are to love one another.
By this all people will know that you are my disciples, if you
have love for one another."
John 13:34-35

In our current society the word "love" has lost meaning. Flippantly, it is thrown out in regard to any preference and carelessly spoken to gain affection from another. However, when we truly love something it is expressed through our actions. Our choices always reveal our true affections. This scripture reveals that our love for God will be evidenced by our love for others. Love always moves us to action. Jesus sets this example for us through His death. His love for us moved Him to respond to our need. And in this passage, we see that we are to love as He has loved. We are to love whether it is deserved or not. We respond to need, not because we have been given reason by the person to do so, but because Christ responded to our need without reason.

We are a people full of self-love. We seek retaliation towards others rather than making allowances for the inevitable faults of others. We seek pleasure and comfort while we ignore the brokenness around us. We hear of sorrow and suffering yet are indifferent toward it because it does not directly affect us. We will be known by the way we live, not by what we say.

Is it possible we live incongruently with our words because we have failed to truly grasp the grace of God ourselves? I believe too many people who claim to be Christians have missed it, so they certainly can't live like they have received it. As self-proclaimed believers we profess Christ and His love, yet we do not live in light of it as often. When we act unloving and indifferent, we give the lost ones nothing to desire. Why would they want anything we have to offer when we are consistently unsatisfied, envious, spiteful, and argumentative? Love is expressed through self-denial, patience, courage, and grace. It's the kindness of the Lord that leads us to repentance (Rom. 2:4), and it will be our kindness that leads others to Him as well. Do you want to make a difference in this world for the cause of Christ? Then love! There is nothing that will have a greater effect.

Listen, it's not just about showing love, but having love. When we serve out of pity or obligation, it is evident to those we are serving. That's not love, and the ones we are serving know it. Matthew Henry says it like this, "Our love to one another must be free and ready, laborious and expensive, constant and persevering; it must be love *to the souls* one of another."[1] Love is a way of life that flows from a transformed heart. By our love they will know whose we are, and our God will be glorified!

Song of Worship: "Waste It All" by United Pursuit

DAY NINETEEN

Beauty in the Night

"Yet God my King is from old, working salvation in the midst of the earth ... Yours is the day, yours also the night ..."
Psalm 74:12, 16

What a wonderful truth by which we might prop ourselves up. Although our God may seem hidden, nevertheless He is working. We all experience times of uncertainty and distress, and it is not uncommon in this life that our hearts become disturbed within us. There are times it seems grief and anxiety as well as fear and loneliness nag at us wanting relief. During these times, our faith can be shaken and we can find ourselves in a season that feels like it will never end. But it is also in these moments we can experience comfort, joy, hope and assurance, deeper than we've ever known them before. He is in the day and also in the night. I want us to consider two truths today that can quiet our minds in our moments of helplessness.

The first truth is: Our God is the great I Am, the Ancient of

Days, and the King of old. He was God then. He is God now. He will forever be God. The One who satisfied the longings of the people of old will satisfy you now. He who brought them out of darkness and broke away the chains is sure to deliver you and overwhelm that which binds you. The One who released them from the foolishness of their sinful ways will also liberate you from your hardness of heart. You can be assured of your I Am. He has not left you alone to formulate your own deliverance.

The second truth is this: The God who commands nature to be still is the God who walks with you. The One who speaks and the winds and waves obey is the same One who offers to be your refuge. He who has has turned seas into dry land and brought water from the rocks, that is the God who has made a promise to be with you and to take care of you. So, you can rest assured that He will make good on His promises, even in the midst of seasons when it seems He is no where to be found. His actions may not come like we expect them to and His presence may be in the whisper rather than the earthquake, wind, or fire (1 Kings 19:9-12), but He has reasons wiser than our own that we can trust.

In your moments of helplessness, admit where you are and lean on our God. Oh, how we fight to deny our brokenness, while failing to realize that our brokenness is actually God's grace in our lives. For by it, we are more likely to turn Him. It's the broken pieces in us that bring us to Him. It's through our brokenness we come to know Him in ways deeper than we ever could without it. I know a godly woman, strong in faith, named Karon Castleberry who once put it this way,

"Some things, like the stars, you can only see in the dark."

It's true that in this life we will have trouble, but it is also equally true that our God will ultimately overcome that trouble. Take heart, my friend, and joy as you marvel at the stars.

Song of Worship: "God Indeed" by Amanda Rucker*

*To listen to this singer/songwriter original, visit www.graciouslybroken.com/gb-music

DAY TWENTY

"For it is by grace you have been saved through faith. And this is not of your own doing; it is the gift of God, not a result of works, so that no one may boast."
Ephesians 2:8-9

Oh, the freedom you can know if you would just rest in this truth. You can't buy your way into heaven. You don't deserve such grace and you could never earn it through any good works of your own. Although this might seem like an offense, in reality, when we grasp this, its beauty captivates our hearts.

Through our acceptance of it, we have been given a new identity that is unshaken by circumstances, failures, or the opinion of men. We no longer have to exhaust ourselves in an attempt to gain that which has already been given. He gives so great a grace, free and unearned, and a mercy that is accessible and inexhaustible!

Salvation is not to be striven for, but to be rested in. Now, don't get me wrong, we strive to live out of this beautiful grace we've been given, but the grace itself is a gift – a gift we are to abide in as we walk out the calling we have received (Eph. 4:1).

So then the next question is, what is the call? Though we were dead in sin, we have been made alive in Christ (Eph. 2:5). But for what reason? Look to Ephesians 2:7, "... so that in the coming ages he might show the immeasurable riches of his grace in kindness toward us in Christ Jesus."

Dear fellow believer, we have been saved, not for our own ease, but for His glory. We have been saved so that others might hear of His kindness toward us and see His kindness towards them as well. Our hope is that they would come to know that God has spoken a better word to them than they have ever heard before (Heb. 12:24). This word declares that there is hope and healing available, and that salvation is obtainable - but not through their own efforts - only by the gift of the finished work of Christ. By way of His death and resurrection, Christ took on our sin and shame, accepted the punishment of death we were due, and gave us the promise of eternal life through His resurrection victory over death.

There is no better word to be spoken, not only to ourselves, but to others who might hear it, be saved through it, and in turn, be a witness for it. It's all about His goodness, not ours.

Song of Worship: "Greatest Love" by Amanda Rucker*

*To listen to this singer/songwriter original, visit www.graciouslybroken.com/gb-music

DAY TWENTY-ONE

Loving the Lie

"He feeds on ashes; a deluded heart has led him astray, and he cannot deliver himself or say, 'Is there not a lie in my right hand?'"
Isaiah 44:20

How often we seek to dine off of delights which only ruin us. The deceptions in our hearts lead us to devote our lives to lies. We charm ourselves with things we think will be to our advantage, yet they only tether us to false hopes. Their reward is, at best, temporary. The gratification found in their obtainment, fleeting.

We look to that which *we* can create, to save us. We seek power and position to ensure our security, only to have our confidence wiped-out when the job is lost or the promotion is given to someone else. We pursue love through sex or the praise of man simply to have our souls crushed by rejection. We seek to define our worth through our spouse, our kids, our friends, or our social status and are left feeling lacking when we don't seem to measure up to their expectations. All of these things leave us starving for affection and weak from empty pursuits.

We know we are missing something. The emptiness we feel whispers to the certainty of it. So we go back to the drawing board, thinking that satisfaction must be found in some other combination. The quest continues, and the emptiness deepens. Without having the awareness of mind to consider that what we are holding so tightly may be a lie, we crumble.

We were created for a relationship with God, but our sin has severed that relationship and left a chasm of desolation in its wake. Instead of turning to the One who formed us, we seek to mend the brokenness we feel with things that are broken themselves. We somehow know the objects of our affection will eventually leave us empty and longing for more, however, we love the lie. Can I just tell you today that, in Christ, our God offers us a security that is unshakable. He offers an unending love that flows from His character, not our goodness. In Him we find worth. We find it in Him, not in any merit we possess, but in what He was willing to pay for us. Everything else that offers fulfillment is a lie.

Song of Worship: "Graves into Gardens" by Brandon Lake & Elevation Worship

DAY TWENTY-TWO

Hiding Place

"Your testimonies are my heritage forever, for they are the joy of my heart... You are my hiding place and my shield; I hope in your word."
Psalm 119:111, 114

Our confidence is found in His Word. Through it, He has revealed His heart and His intentions toward us. Those revelations help position our hearts.

The Psalmist let the word of God be considered actual evidence of what was to come. He established his life on it's foundation. As a result, he could testify with all assurance that God was his hiding place and shield against the pursuit of his enemy.

We, too, can have assurance in times of temptation and trials. Our enemy pursues us seeking to taint any evidence of Christ's life in us. He aims to steal our joy and wonder and destroy all hope and resolve, yet we know that God's testimonies are our heritage. His testimonies are our birthright as adopted sons and daughters. We comfort ourselves with the protection and defense found in God alone and hold fast to who He has revealed Himself to be. In Matthew Henry's Commentary he states, "Now God was both of these to him, a hiding place to preserve him *from* danger and a shield to preserve him *in* danger, his life from death and his soul from sin" (italics added for emphasis).[1]

Do you feel as though you are going to collapse in these days of trouble? Do you feel like you are drowning under the waters of your grief and sorrow? Blanket yourself in the testimonies of your God. He is your hiding place, and His offer to you is rest: "Come to me, all who labor and are heavy laden, and I will give you rest" (Matt. 11:28). He understands. He knows the burden is too heavy for us to carry alone.

Are you unable to believe you will ever be able to lay aside the weight of sin that so easily entangles you? Are you struggling well but slowly sinking into exhaustion? Hold fast to your shield for "he will not let you be tempted beyond what you can bear. But when you are tempted, he will also provide a way out so that you can endure it" (1 Cor. 10:13, NIV).

We have so many assurances in Christ. We will not experience them all this side of heaven, but we know and are certain that they are ours to come! Until then, let Him and His Word be your hiding place in times of trial.

Song of Worship: "Hidden" by Will Reagan & United Pursuit

DAY TWENTY-THREE

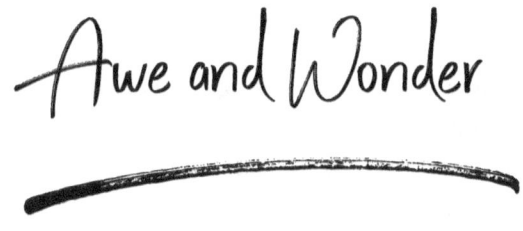
Awe and Wonder

"There is no fear in love, but perfect love casts out fear. For fear has to do with punishment, and whoever fears has not been perfected in love."
1 John 4:18

Often, large portions of our lives are driven by fear. We don't like to admit it, but it is true. Many of our everyday insecurities are rooted in fear. Examples of common everyday insecurities are the fear of being unlovable, the fear of not being good enough, and the fear of not having what we need. Our experiences in life sometimes lead us to believe things about ourselves, God, and others that are not necessarily true. In our minds we may declare false statements like the following:

- "My father left me, so there must be something wrong with me."
- "My closest friend betrayed me, so I can no longer trust anyone."

- "My child died, so God cannot be a loving or good God."
- "I've done so much wrong and hurt so many people. There's no way God could love me now."

Examples like these are unending, but do you see how fear initially begins to creep into our hearts? Today's scripture indicates that where love is perfect, fear is expelled. My questions, then, are as follows: What is perfect love? And how is perfect love able to cast out the fear in my life?

There is only one place we will find perfect love, and that is in God. His love is pure and selfless all the time, and was not earned or deserved. Romans 5:6 echoes this when it says, "For while we were still weak, at the right time Christ died for the ungodly." I believe many of us have not experienced true life transformation solely because the depth of the love of God has not been realized in our lives. Whether it be because of justification, comparison, or pride, we usually tend toward one of the following extremes or the other, which both hinder us from realizing the depth of His love. We either fail to realize that we are the ungodly ones being referred to in Romans 5:6, or we consider the grace of God to be insufficient for our particular sinfulness.

When we understand that our God loved us at our worst and met us in our sinfulness, the fear of His judgement falls away. Our fear is replaced with awe and wonder, and our hearts are stirred to love the One who loved us first. And listen, for the one who thinks they have no need for the love of God, you've never been more wrong. I have some news for you. But the good news is only good news when we first acknowledge the bad news. So, the bad news is we all desperately need to realize the depth of God's love if we ever want to feel whole, and not even one of us deserve it. But the good news is He gave it anyway. No matter who you are, He knows you and is offering His love to you if you'll only decide to receive it.

When we come to a place of understanding where we begin to stand in awe and wonder of His love, our fears begin to dissipate. The lies and fear begin to vanish as they're overshadowed by the light of the free, yet costly grace given us in Christ.

Song of Worship: "Holy Ground" by Passion

DAY TWENTY-FOUR

"Shout, and sing for joy, O inhabitant of Zion, for great in your midst is the Holy One of Israel."
Isaiah 12:6

Our circumstances, trials, and struggles often try to keep our souls from celebrating God. However, there are greater reasons still to magnify Him. All of us, though undeserving, have been offered salvation and deliverance. In Christ, we have been rescued from the penalty of our sin and have been given a new life that is eternal. Through Him we have peace with God and comfort in His love.

Look with me at Luke 19:37: "When [Jesus] came near . . . the whole crowd of disciples began joyfully to praise God in loud voices" (NIV).

I read this and thought about how there were certainly some in the crowd who were going through seasons of suffering, whether it be from sickness or abuse. Some were facing trials – possibly trials that came because their child walked away from the faith, or trials that came because of lost financial stability. There were almost definitely ones in the crowd battling fear, insecurities, and doubt, and others in the crowd who were struggling with sin and temptation. Yet . . . they sang! Why? What triggered their song?

I believe they sang because they understood their Savior was in their midst. As they remembered all God had done, they couldn't help but sing out their faith about what He would do through His Son! They let their hearts be stirred into song to acknowledge and proclaim His greatness. No matter what you feel, let your soul sing!

Mrs. Charles E. Cowman once wrote, "It is your mission, tested and tried one, to walk out on the stage of this world and reveal to all earth and heaven that music is not in conditions, not in the things, not in externals, but the music of life is in your own soul."[1]

Song of Worship: "New Song" by Amanda Rucker[*]

[*]To listen to this singer/songwriter original, visit www.graciouslybroken.com/gb-music

DAY TWENTY-FIVE

Awake, O Sleeper

> *"But when anything is exposed by the light, it becomes visible, for anything that becomes visible is light. Therefore it says: 'Awake, O sleeper, and arise from the dead, and Christ will shine on you.' Look carefully then how you walk, not as unwise but as wise, making the best use of the time..."*
> *Ephesians 5:13-16*

In this passage we are given a call to live and behave as those who have been saved by God. In accordance with His love, God through Christ has forgiven our sin, and because of that, we are to imitate Him.

He goes on to remind us that although we were at one time people of the darkness, we are now people of light in Christ, and so we should walk in that manner. We should not only put away the foolish deeds of darkness but expose them for what they are.

How do we do that? In our culture today, we are surrounded by darkness and it is easy to settle into grey areas. We error greatly when we call out the sin in the lives of others all while justifying the sin in our own. We can often use the knowledge of another's sin struggles to make us feel better about our own. We may not verbally say it, but our hearts say, "At least I don't do *that*."

We forget that in this passage Paul is writing to believers, not unbelievers. Far too often we want to argue over the condition of our country and talk about the audacity of the sins of unbelievers, while all along we are as comfortable in our areas of sin as they are in theirs. We proclaim to be followers of Christ yet live as the world. We have to look inward with honesty. We won't be able to see clearly to help them if we won't look clearly at our own self (Matt. 7:2-5), and we certainly won't show compassion for them while doing it if we never see how much we actually struggle in areas of sin ourselves.

Listen, through this passage the Holy Spirit is calling us out of our spiritual slumber. We need to make the best use of what little time we are given, so wake up! Let the light of His truth shine in the dark, hidden places of your own life. Then as the light takes over your life more and more, others might see that light and desire Him to light their darkness, too.

Song of Worship: "Light Shine In" by Jacob Sooter & Vertical Worship

DAY TWENTY-SIX

Undeserved Kindness

"For all have sinned and fall short of the glory of God, and are justified by his grace as a gift, through the redemption that is in Christ Jesus..."
Romans 3:23-24

I have a passion for wretched people to come to know how great the love of God is for them. If you are asking yourself, "Did she just call me a wretch?" I want you to know, without a doubt, that yes, I did. And I pray that you hear me when I say that not only is it right that I refer to each of us in that way, but it is to our benefit that we acknowledge that truth for ourselves. For only when we have a right estimation of ourselves, does the great love of God, which is evidenced by His grace given us, become so amazing.

Scripture tells us in Matthew 5:3, "Blessed are the poor in spirit, for theirs is the kingdom of heaven." This scripture isn't saying, "Blessed are the ones who think they are okay." Neither is it saying, "Blessed are the ones who know they aren't perfect, but at least they aren't as bad as the next person." It's not even saying, "Blessed are the ones who struggle but think they will be okay once they buckle down and try a little harder." No! This scripture is referring to the one who knows they have absolutely nothing to offer a Holy God in and of themselves.

This is so important because we will never be overwhelmed by the love of God if we continue to believe that we either don't need it or that we somehow deserve it. It is only when we realize how great of a need we have for Him, and just how unworthy we are to receive Him, that the beauty of His freely-given love will inflame our hearts with purpose. It is only then, in wonder and awe, that we will be able to sing the old hymn, "Amazing grace - how sweet the sound - that saved a wretch like me!"[1]

In Romans 7, Paul is being transparent with us by confessing that he doesn't do the things he wants to do, but instead, he does the things he hates. Can you relate? I can. He is frustrated and tired of the battle that wages against him. Listen to what he says in verse 24, "Wretched man that I am! Who will deliver me from this body of death?" Paul wasn't trying to excuse the sin in his life. He was acknowledging the reality of his wretchedness.

What I find interesting is what that acknowledgement motivated inside of him. Look at verse 25: "Thanks be to God through Jesus Christ our Lord!" The acknowledgement of his brokenness led his soul to worship the One who died to mend it.

Will you be brave enough to acknowledge your wretchedness and brokenness today so your soul can begin to truly worship?...for "blessed are the poor in spirit, for theirs is the kingdom of heaven" (Matt. 5:3).

Song of Worship: "Broken Vessels (Amazing Grace)" by
                Hillsong Worship

DAY TWENTY-SEVEN

A Life Exhausted

"But I do not account my life of any value nor as precious to myself, if only I may finish my course and the ministry that I received from the Lord Jesus, to testify to the gospel of the grace of God."
Acts 20:24

When we truly see what has been afforded to us in Jesus, when we come to understand, however vaguely, the depth of His love, the whole aim of our lives change.

Through Paul's testimony we see that this life is not about our comfort or convenience. He was determined to follow Christ in spite of the affliction that awaited him. He understood that, when it came to God, he had no right to himself. He found comfort in the grace given to him through the gospel, and in turn, he positioned himself to live his life in response to it.

True Christianity is not an "I'm okay - you're okay - do what feels good to you" type of life. God has not saved us so we would continue to serve ourselves. He says if you want to follow Me, then deny yourself (Matt. 16:24-26). Put to death the things of your flesh and live in light of the price paid for you (Rom. 8:12-13).

Paul grasped this in a way that changed everything in his life. His desires, affections, and appetites no longer carried ultimate weight in his life. His only aim was to complete the task God had given him, which was to "to testify to the gospel of the grace of God" (Acts 20:24).

Our task is the same. It may be carried out differently in each of our lives, but still, it is the same. Listen, we all exhaust our lives for something. At the end of your life, will what you exhausted it for matter? I don't know about you, but I want to exhaust my life for something that will outlast my time here. Oh, what grace! I don't deserve it, but by God's grace, I will proclaim it.

Song of Worship: "Offering" by Third Day

DAY TWENTY-EIGHT

Compelling Grace

"All this from God, who through Christ reconciled us to himself and gave us the ministry of reconciliation ... For our sake he made him to be sin who knew no sin, so that in him we might become the righteousness of God."
2 Corinthians 5:18, 21

In Christ, our greatest need has been met. We who were once separated from God have been reconciled to Him through the grace given to us in Christ. This is great news for us. Listen, there is a God and we have all sinned against Him and are thereby separated from Him. The payment due for our sin is death, and we are entitled to pay up.

But what great grace we have been given! The Son of God humbled Himself to human form and paid the debt of death in full for all who would believe and turn to Him. The sins of those who believe are no longer counted against them. How wonderful a grace!

First Corinthians 5:21 says, "For our sake he made him to

be sin who knew no sin, so that in him we might become the righteousness of God." He who never sinned, willingly took my sin upon His shoulders. He bore my shame, went to the cross for my sin, and took the full measure of God's wrath upon Himself, so that I might not have to for eternity. He gave me His right standing with God, and now I am looked upon by God as one who has been declared righteous.

How crazy is that? When my heart begins to fathom the depths He has gone to in order that I could be brought back to Him, there is a holy passion ignited within me to not only live my life in love to Him, but to share with others what a love I have found.

And what a compelling love it is! It is one that stirs our hearts toward the Giver of such a costly grace. We will never be perfect, but as we reflect on His grace toward us and all that it cost Him, it ought to move our hearts to mourn when we live in a way that cheapens it, tramples over it, or completely disregards it.

We are called to carry the message of this grace. We are told that Christ has entrusted to us this message of reconciliation. We are His representatives and He is making His appeal to others through our changed lives, so that they might be reconciled to God as well. What message are people receiving from your life?

Song of Worship: "More than the Nails" by Philip Melton*

*To listen to this singer/songwriter original, visit www.graciouslybroken.com/gb-music

DAY TWENTY-NINE

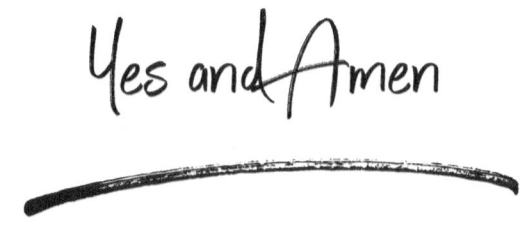

*"For all the promises of God find their Yes in him. That is
why it is through him that we utter our
Amen to God for his glory."*
2 Corinthians 1:20

Everyday we are faced with something we have no control over or that we don't understand. However, these situations don't prove that God is wrong, unloving, or unable to be trusted. We need only to look at the cross to see that His wisdom is inconceivable. Who would imagine that our hope would come through Christ's death? It doesn't really make sense that life is found in death or that victory lies in submission.

Can I just be honest with you? You will never have all your answers to the whys, because His ways are far higher than yours. That's the reason we must learn to trust Him. We must learn to trust in His love for us and in His sovereignty over everything. We must learn to trust in and stand firm on His truths, especially when they are not easy to believe in the midst of our circumstances.

Amen - We believe You God, and we declare that You are faithful and reliable. We believe that You will bring us out of our distress in Your perfect timing, for You have redeemed us, and You will save us. We are Yours, and You are ours!

We fasten our confidence not to what we can see, but to who He is. In the midst of sorrow and discouragement, as we are waiting for the answers, we take Him at His word. And it is during our suffering, as we stand in confident expectation of the hope we have in Christ, that we reflect His beauty and His glory to a watching world.

When life seems pointless and no one else is around, we command our souls to say "Amen" to the truth that our God is always there. He is our ever-present help - an exceeding help! When we feel as though we are drowning in grief, we remember our God, the God of all comfort, the One who sustains us, and we say "Amen," because we know that though the waters rise, they won't sweep over us. When disappointment and betrayal attempt to harden our hearts, we say "Amen" as we remember to live in the grace and love that we ourselves have received. And His grace will move in our hearts and motivate us to forgive as we have been forgiven and love as we have been loved by Him. Whatever you are facing, utter your amen.

Song of Worship: "Prophecy Your Promise" by Bryan & Katie Torwalt & Jesus Culture

DAY THIRTY

You Are Mine

"But now thus says the Lord, he who created you ... he who formed you ... 'Fear not, for I have redeemed you; I have called you by name, you are mine. When you pass through the waters, I will be with you; and through the rivers, they shall not overwhelm you; when you walk through fire you shall not be burned, and the flame shall not consume you. For I am the Lord your God, the Holy One of Israel, your Savior."
Isaiah 43:1-3

To me, this is one of the sweetest passages in Scripture as He declares, "You are mine." When I read these words, I think of my kid. Countless times I have told him the reason I do something is "because you're mine." "I love you, because you're mine." "I'm going with you, because you're mine." "I'm going to protect you, because you're mine." Words like these are spoken out of the great love and affection I have for him. I cherish him. He is special to me. He matters to me. What hurts him, hurts me. When he cries, I want to comfort him.

So, when I read these words in Isaiah, I get a profound sense that God feels the same way about me. It's as if He is saying to me, "Amanda, don't worry, you're Mine . . . I'm going to go with you, because you're Mine . . . Don't be afraid of those waters. I won't let them sweep over you, you're Mine . . . That fire, it won't consume you, you're Mine . . . I know you're feeling discouraged and distressed, but take heart My love, and let Me comfort you, because you're Mine!"

You are Mine! What a difference three words can make! Because we are His, we don't have to fear. Because we are His, we can be assured that although the rivers surge and the fires blaze, we are not overwhelmed and we are not consumed. He is our Lord. He is our Savior.

Listen, we are all subject to give way under the pressures of life. When we feel as though we are going to completely collapse under the weight of our sin, remember Christ. Even the Psalmist relates, "For evils have encompassed me beyond number; my iniquities have overtaken me, and I cannot see; they are more than the hairs of my head; my heart fails me" (Ps. 40:12). We all feel it, don't we? But listen, like the Psalmist, we too can state with all confidence, "My flesh and my heart may fail, but God is the strength of my heart and my portion forever" (Ps. 73:26).

Take heart! Hold fast to the Lord, for He is holding fast to you! You are His.

Song of Worship: "Do it Again" by Elevation Worship

DAY THIRTY-ONE

Invitation to the Thirsty

"Come, everyone who thirsts, come to the waters; and he who has no money, come, buy and eat! Come, buy ... without money and without price. Why do you spend your money for that which is not bread, and your labor for that which does not satisfy?"
Isaiah 55:1-2

Just like in this passage of Scripture, I believe God is calling out to you today to try to get your attention. Open your heart and listen to Him saying, "Hey, you! Yeah, you! Are you thirsty? Are you hurting? Are you broken? Are you overwhelmed and at the end of yourself? Are you looking for something more? Come, drink, and be satisfied! You don't have to keep spending money on what isn't filling you up. You don't have to keep chasing what isn't satisfying. Come! Do you have regrets, and have you made mistakes? It's okay. Come! In Me, you will find forgiveness. Are you unhappy or disappointed? Are you grieving the loss of a loved one or maybe the loss of a dream? Come! Trade your sorrow for the joy found in a relationship with Me. Because of My everlasting kindness, I will have compassion on you. Come!"

Listen, His invitation is to you, and it demands a response. What will your response be today? It will require movement on your part. It takes faith, which means we come in spite of our fear of the unknown.

Maybe you need to make a shift back toward Christ. Have you have accepted his gift of salvation, but at some point turned away from following Him to go your own way? It isn't always a big sin that leads people away. Maybe for you it's simply fear that keeps you from turning back to Him. Or, perhaps, you have never officially responded to His invitation to come to Him in the first place. If that is you, surrender your life to the One who gave His for you.

Either way, hear God saying to you, "I have blotted out your transgressions like a cloud and your sins like mist; return to me, for I have redeemed you" (Isa. 44:22).

I'm reminded of what the Lord said through His prophet Jeremiah, ". . . for my people have committed two evils: they have forsaken me, the fountain of living waters, and hewed out cisterns for themselves, broken cisterns that can hold no water" (Jer. 2:13). The question isn't whether you are thirsty or not; The question is whether you are going to turn to the fountain of living water or keep going back to those broken, empty wells. Which will it be for you?

Song of Worship: "Living Water" by Lauren Dunn & Gateway Worship

DAY THIRTY-TWO

Give Thanks

"Oh give thanks to the Lord, for he is good, for his steadfast love endures forever!"
Psalm 107:1

Sometimes we just need to stop and cultivate a thankful heart. I know it can be hard to keep a heart of gratitude, especially when you've been through situations no one should have to experience. It's really hard to be grateful when it seems like your world is crashing in around you or when your marriage is failing, your kid is using drugs, or you're dealing with the aftermath of abuse. It's really hard to be grateful to God in moments like these when you find yourself wondering if He is even there.

I remember this one particular day when I was reflecting back on a certain situation I had endured. Through prayer, I was trying to make sense of God's role in that circumstance. During my time with Him, He opened my eyes to see more than just the evil I had experienced. He began to reveal everything I had escaped. He revealed all that could've happened or almost happened but didn't. All of a sudden, I was filled with gratitude for how He protected me from what would have certainly been too much for me to handle and from the extra evils that couldn't be turned and used for my good and His glory later. Only He can decipher those things.

My gratitude continued to grow as God began to show me how all of the experiences He allowed had a major role in making me who I am today. He showed me that it was my brokenness that helped me recognize my need for Jesus. Without it, would I have ever turned to Him? I don't think I would have. Even with the ongoing struggles I face, and the sins that so easily trip me up, God has shown me that those "thorns in my flesh" are the very things that keep me dependent on God. Am I happy for my struggles? No. Am I grateful that He will use them to help me know Him more intimately? Yes.

Listen, we all have a choice. We can either let our past and present hurts pull us away from God - which only fuels our addictions, fears, and resentments - or we can allow them to draw us into the heart and attention of God so He can transform them into something good.

I'll never forget these moments when God began to open my eyes to it all. I was driving in my car and remember responding, "Okay then. Just don't let it be for nothing." And to this day, He hasn't. He has been faithful to me and a good steward of my pain.

Join me in letting Psalm 30:11-12 stir your heart to give thanks today: "You have turned for me my mourning into dancing; you have loosed my sackcloth and clothed me with gladness, that my glory may sing your praise and not be silent. O Lord my God, I will give thanks to you forever!"

Song of Worship: "We Dance" by Steffany Gretzinger & Bethel Music

DAY THIRTY-THREE

Like Those Who Dream

"When the Lord restored the fortunes of Zion, we were like those who dream. Then our mouth was filled with laughter, and our tongue with shouts of joy; then they said among the nations, 'The Lord has done great things for them.' The Lord has done great things for us; we are glad."
Psalm 126:1-2

We have all been disappointed by hope at some point in our lives. For me, many years of my life were spent searching for something to make me feel okay with myself. Despite my vast search, all my efforts seemed to only deepen my depravity. I don't believe I am all that different from you or anyone else. We all know there is something lacking in us, something missing. We try to mask it in the best ways we know how, but those masks always end up slipping eventually, and we are left with the wreckage of yet another vain pursuit. We are too often afraid to be authentic, even when the masks have drained us and made us lose ourselves behind them.

We try to cover up and hide our sin. We want to give off the appearance of perfection, of strength, of superiority. We want to come across as the nice one so that others will love us, or we use intimidation, daring anyone to get close.

Whatever your mask may be, the purpose is the same. We use them for self-protection - to try and control how God and others see us. However, instead of protecting us, they merely serve to enslave us. The void gets deeper, the pain gets greater, and there's one more voice echoing in our minds telling us how worthless we are.

Oh, but listen: Hope has come. Love has come. Salvation has come. The longing can be filled. And when we finally experience it, it seems like a dream. Love undeserved – freedom through the work of Another. Crazy, isn't it? Where others have mocked and jeered at our misfortune, they will now marvel at our freedom. We glory in our Jesus for He loves us and has given us a way out from under our masks. Take a moment to let this sink in and be glad!

Our liberation from hiding ought to seem too good to be true, and the awe of it so overwhelming that there is nothing to do but to laugh and sing for joy. For the waiting has made the arrival sweet.

Song of Worship: "My Soul Magnifies the Lord" by Chris Tomlin

DAY THIRTY-FOUR

Intense but Measured

"We are afflicted in every way, but not crushed; perplexed, but not driven to despair; persecuted, but not forsaken; struck down, but not destroyed; always carrying in the body the death of Jesus, so that the life of Jesus may also be manifested in our bodies."
2 Corinthians 4:8-10

I remember a time early in my recovery journey when the obsession to use was overwhelming. I couldn't seem to get any relief. I was desperate not to return to my addiction, but my strength to keep fighting seemed to be evaporating. I felt tormented by the cravings and plagued by the lies that I would never be anything more than an addict.

I recall reaching out to one person after another for help, but no one was there. I finally reached out to my dad and he picked me up and drove me around all day. We went nowhere in particular and said almost nothing to each other. We just drove. I spent all day enduring overwhelming emotions I felt would never end.

However, despite my emotions, versions of today's verse played through my mind on repeat. "I am pressed on every side, but I am not destroyed." Over and over it would pass through my mind in different ways. "Though I'm pressed on all sides, I'm not destroyed . . . Though all sides are pressing in, I won't be destroyed . . ." I did not know at the time that my mom's friend had been praying this exact verse over me that day.

Now listen, I am not saying that I experienced anything nearly as awful as what Paul experienced. All I'm saying is that I have experienced moments where it felt like too much, moments when I couldn't understand why, and times when it felt like I had been forgotten. I believe many of us experience periods in our lives when it seems like God is nowhere to be found. These periods usually come during seasons when our hope has been trampled, life has left us baffled, or when the present anxieties feel so much like a plague that we feel knocked down and like we have nothing left to give.

Within this passage, however, we are reminded that although we will experience times like these, there is a limit to them. Though they may be intense, they are measured. I pray you would know today that no matter what comes, you are not alone, and our Jesus understands. So, "let us then with confidence draw near to the throne of grace, that we may receive mercy and find grace to help in time of need" (Heb. 4:16).

Hear me today: You may be pressed on all sides, but you are not without hope. No matter how alone you feel, He is there. Your hardship may last for a season, but joy will be on the other side.

Song of Worship: "There was Jesus" by Zach Williams & Dolly Parton

DAY THIRTY-FIVE

Carry Your Cross

"Then Jesus told his disciples, 'If anyone would come after me, let him deny himself and take up his cross and follow me.'"
Matthew 16:24

The love of Christ is a beautiful comfort for any who would believe in Him and receive it in faith, and we have great consolation in salvation through Him. However, far too often, while we seek to enjoy the comforts of following Christ, we reject the call that accompanies the comforts. We don't mind following Him as much as we are willing, just as long as He doesn't ask us to surrender what is most precious to us or ask us to step too far out of our comfort zones. We are so accustomed to instant gratification that the idea of self-denial seems ludicrous.

I hear often, "God wants me to be happy." Can I just tell you that your happiness is not His ultimate goal for your life? His desire is that you would conform your life to His. His desire is that you would live and love and respond in such a way that when people see you, they would know to glorify Him.

God is very clear in these verses about what following after Him will cost us - *all* of us. Self-denial and self-sacrifice are not just for the "elite" Christ-followers, but for *all* Christ-followers. Basically, He is saying, "If you want to follow Me, then follow Me. Deny yourself and take up your own cross so you can follow where I lead."

The Gospel of Luke describes the cost of discipleship like this: "For which of you, desiring to build a tower, does not first sit down and count the cost . . . any of you who does not renounce all that he has cannot be my disciple" (Lk. 14:28, 33). Matthew Henry's Commentary speaks on this verse by saying, "It is as if Christ has said, 'If any of the people that are not my disciples, be steadfastly minded to come to me, and if you that are, be in like manner minded to adhere to me, it is upon these terms, these and no other; you must *follow me* in sufferings as well as in other things, and therefore when you sit down to count the cost, reckon upon it.'"[1]

Listen, we shouldn't dictate to God what we will and won't do once we have received His salvation and made the commitment to follow Him. We shouldn't put stipulations on it as though we are doing Him a favor by following Him. He did us a favor by offering us salvation. We have good reason to live as He lived and go where He leads.

We don't get to gauge the definition of holiness by the standard of our culture or the opinion of any other. His life, His Word, and His way are our standard. We measure ourselves by Him. As you consider this today, I want you to remember that Jesus is not asking you to bear your cross alone. He is just asking you to take it up. Is there an area of life you're holding back that needs to be surrendered today?

Song of Worship: "Carry Me Through" by Dave Barnes

DAY THIRTY-SIX

Anchor for the Soul

*"We have this as a sure and steadfast anchor of the soul,
a hope that enters into the inner place behind the curtain,
where Jesus has gone as a forerunner on our behalf..."*
Hebrews 6:19-20

We often seek security in things that are ever-changing. We attach our identities to our job, our spouse, our kids, our friends, our possessions, or even our level of education. We look for acceptance in man's approval. We look for salvation in our right behaviors. We know the right answers, but I think the application of them is a little trickier for us to grasp.

This world has a way of tossing us about and knocking us off course like a ship at sea during a storm. Temptations seek to lure us away, while suffering attempts to shipwreck our faith. Therefore, it is vital that we anchor our hope on that which never changes and is not dependent on us.

The author of Hebrews is clear that there is a sure and steadfast anchor for our souls. It's an anchor that rests solely on the integrity and promises of our God. The basis of our hope is the good news of the love of God, displayed through the cross of Christ. We can speak with confidence and certainty, not because of anything to do with us, but because of the nature of God and His ability and willingness to save.

I want us to see two life-altering truths about hope. First, look at Psalm 107 and you will see that hope positions us for restoration. When all seemed lost, the people of God turned to Him and cried out in hope. It was their cry to the Lord that initiated the shift from their trouble to their rescue.

The second thing we need to realize is that when our faith is placed in lesser things, our hope comes and goes with the tides of life. There is nothing that holds our hope secure. But when we anchor ourselves to the truth of His love for us, we find strength and support through life's uncertainties. So, not only does hope position us for restoration, it is also what sustains us through adversity.

In the midst of what seems to be a season of constant failures and setbacks, when you are tempted to lose all hope of you or anything in your life ever being any different, don't allow your feelings to define your expectations of what God will do. Anchor your soul to the deep love He has for you, cry out to Him, and cling to who you know Him to be.

Song of Worship: "How Deep the Father's Love For Us" by Stuart Townend

DAY THIRTY-SEVEN

The Purity of Conscience

"... how much more will the blood of Christ, who through the eternal Spirit offered himself without blemish to God, purify our conscience from dead works to serve the living God."
Hebrews 9:14

In Old Testament times, the people did not have the kind of access to God we do now. One time a year the high priest would enter the Holy of Holies and offer a sin sacrifice for the people. This external ritual had no power to save them from their slavery to sin or to purify their consciences from the guilt of their sin. The imperfection of the sacrifice merely served to buy a year reprieve in the sight of God. However, this sacrifice foreshadowed the hope that was to come. God would one day send a Savior to be the fulfillment of all things promised. Christ would come to be both a new and better High Priest and the ultimate Sacrifice. Those who would hope in this new High Priest would no longer be separated from God, and what the blood of animals ultimately failed to do, the blood of Christ would bring to completion. There would no longer be a curtain dividing the holiness of God from man, and there would no longer be a need to go through human priests to be made right with God because Jesus would become our Great High Priest forever. He is now the mediator for the people of God, and through His blameless life, sacrificial death, and conquering resurrection, Christ proved to be the perfect and ultimate Sacrifice. He took our sin upon Himself, died in our place, rose from the hold of death, and now stands before God as our intermediary. In Christ our redemption was secured once for all, not by the blood of animals, but by His own divine blood. What the writer of Hebrews is saying here is that if the blood of a mere animal can purify the body temporarily, how much more will the blood of the eternal Christ accomplish?

Have you ever said, "I would love to do this or that for the Lord, but I'm not fit for such service to Him?" Listen, don't miss this. What we see here is that the blood of Jesus is so effective in the purification of our sin that it has the power to cleanse our consciences so that even the sense of guilt is taken away! He not only wipes away our sin, He purifies our conscience when we believe so we are free to serve Him without the added burden of a guilty conscience. The song of worship today is one of my favorites on the subject. I encourage you to take the time to look it up. Listen in such a way that your heart could be gripped anew by the wonder of it all.

Song of Worship: "Nothing but the Blood" by Corey Voss

DAY THIRTY-EIGHT

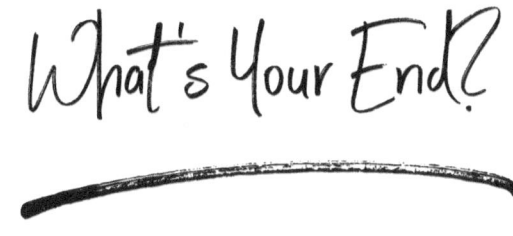

What's Your End?

"... that I may know him and the power of his resurrection ... I press on toward the goal for the prize of the upward call of God in Christ Jesus."
Philippians 3:10, 14

In the first part of Philippians 3, Paul listed all the areas where he had previously placed his assurance. His assurance had been placed in credentials involving who he was and what he had accomplished. This is very similar to what we still do today. I believe it is because we all have an inward need to feel significant, to know that we matter, and to know that we are here for a reason. Paul came to understand, however, that any sort of enduring significance would not be found in those things. He came to believe that the practice of looking to the things of the flesh to give himself value was garbage. Once he came to know Christ, it no longer made sense to him to place his confidence in such things that are here today and gone tomorrow. But let's just be honest with each other. We struggle to get there, don't we? It's not that we think Jesus is a bad addition to our lives; it's just that He isn't necessarily the goal of our lives and we know it.

We have our hearts fixed on the job, the relationship, the acceptance, or the popularity. Every so often the Holy Spirit will open our eyes to see that our only interest in Jesus has been so He would get on board with our pursuits. My prayer for you today is that you would see that Jesus is not the means to some other end, He is *the* end! For what have you been striving? What most often consumes your thought life? And what does how you spend your time reveal about your pursuits?

Solomon, in the book of Ecclesiastes, attempts to enlighten us to the futility of such empty pursuits. Not that everything we chase after is bad, but when those things become the sole aim or importance of our lives, we will, in the end, find them to be worthless. Listen to what he says: "Then I considered all that my hands had done and the toil I had expended in doing it, and behold, all was vanity and a striving after wind, and there was nothing to be gained under the sun" (Ecc. 2:11).

How much time we have wasted chasing after something as elusive as the wind! And even if we are able to attain what we have been striving for, we will still be left wanting. Oh, that we might know the surpassing worth of knowing Christ Jesus our Lord and living for Him completely! Everything else we might gain will be considered a loss in comparison.

Song of Worship: "Worth It All" by Meredith Andrews

DAY THIRTY-NINE

"... let us also lay aside every weight, and sin which clings so closely, and let us run with endurance the race that is set before us, looking to Jesus, the founder and perfecter of our faith, who for the joy that was set before him endured the cross, despising the shame, and is seated at the right hand of the throne of God."
Hebrews 12:1-2

In the chapter previous to this passage, the writer of Hebrews gave testament to some who have gone before us, who in faith persevered through doubt and suffering. He then begins chapter 12 with these words, *"Let us also..."* Let us also lay aside the things that hinder our pursuit of Christ. We all have misplaced affections in our lives that rob God of the affections due Him. It's these misplaced affections that tend to weigh us down and avert us from pushing ahead in our faith. There are things we indulge ourselves with, and justifications we make that cause us to stumble. This passage encourages us, like those of great faith before us, to lay aside all the things that hinder, whether those hindrances are internal emotions like fear, insecurity, doubt, or false beliefs, or whether they are external entanglements like improper relationships or an unhealthy pursuit of social status or financial gain.

The author is reminding us that we each have a race to run, and our race has been marked out for us already. If we want to run well, we must first prepare ourselves for the race by laying aside the things that will get in the way. This is a long distance race that has been set before us, and if we hope to finish it, we have to have grit. We will need fortitude to endure the hardships along the way. We must persist even in the face of rejection, persecution, and suffering. How do we do this? We look to Jesus, the One who began our life of faith and the One who will be the fulfillment of it.

There is no greater example or source of motivation than Jesus Himself. So, we consider Jesus. We consider all He endured on our behalf. He endured rejection, mockery, abuse, and ultimately a horrific death - all for our sake. Let us consider Him further to find out what motivated His endurance and let it be the source of our motivation as well.

So, why did He endure? He endured "for the joy that was set before him" (Heb. 12:2). I believe that the joy set before Him was both the joy of obedience to His Father and the joy of attainment of salvation for us.

Listen, I know it's hard. I know you get tired. I know. But hear me, Jesus knows, too. Look to Him, consider Him, and know that we, too, have a joy awaiting us when we leave this world – a joy that is beyond comparison to anything we could think or imagine. So, fix your eyes on the joy set before you like He did for us, and run your race well!

Song of Worship: "For the Cross" by Bethel Music & Jenn Johnson

DAY FORTY

"For we do not have a high priest who is unable to sympathize with our weaknesses, but one who in every respect has been tempted as we are, yet without sin. Let us then with confidence draw near to the throne of grace, that we may receive mercy and find grace to help in time of need."
Hebrews 4:15-16

I don't know about you, but I relate all too well to Paul when he states in Romans 7:15, "For what I want to do I do not do, but what I hate I do" (NIV). It seems as though my life has been constantly marked by sin struggles. Far too often, I fall prey to the temptations in my life. It's not comfortable to admit this fact, but I've learned that it is not to my benefit to try and pretend otherwise. There have been many times when I've been overcome with grief because of the sin in my life. I would get engtangled in sin again when I willingly chose to walk away from God to pursue other affections. Early on in my Christian walk, such failures would drive me to despair. I would allow my guilt and my shame to prevent me from turning back to the only One who could help me.

What I have learned over the years, though, is that there is a grace that comes with brokenness. It was in my brokenness that I felt the truth of His kindness. It was in brokenness that I experienced His tenderness. It was only in the wake of brokenness that I came to understand the liberating result of His mercy.

This is what I've learned: when there's nowhere else to go and nothing left to do, fall down. I used to think that Jesus was going to hold my failures up as a reason why He could no longer love me. I was so wrong. What I've come to learn is that the One who died for me, is the One who stands in my defense! Hear me, He's not judging us - He's representing us. He is our champion. And what's even more wonderful is He understands. Although He never sinned, He was tempted in every manner, just like us. It was hard for Him, too.

Listen, this understanding changes everything! For it is because of that truth, we are invited to draw near to Him with confidence. Past regrets won't turn Him away; current struggles won't turn Him away; future worries won't turn Him away! There is a throne of grace that we are invited to approach with all boldness and all assurance, and when we do, we will receive the grace we need. What does your heart feel like today? Are you overwhelmed by your sin? Are you consumed with grief? Are you becoming hardened by bitterness? Do you feel crushed by responsibility? Dear friend, fall down. Get on your face before your loving God. Accept the help found at the feet of your Great Defender. He's not mad at you or wearied by you. He loves you and wants you to come to Him. He is for you, not against you.

Song of Worship: "Another in the Fire" by
                Hillsong UNITED

Endnotes

Day 5: Safe Harbor

1. Thayer and Smith, "Greek Lexicon entry for Kardia," *The NAS New Testament Greek Lexicon*, accessed January 15, 2021, https://www.biblestudytools.com/lexicons/greek/nas/kardia.html.

Day 12: But God

1. Jon Bloom, "But God," *Desiring God*, accessed January15, 2021, https://www.desiringgod.org/articles/but-god, used by permission.

Day 14: Fix Your Face

1. Charles Haddon Spurgeon, "The Redeemer's Face Set Like a Flint," *Metropolitan Tabernacle Pulpit, Vol. 47, November 28, 1880*, accessed January 15, 2021, https://www.spurgeon.org/resource-library/sermons/the-redeemers-face-set-like-a-flint/.

Day 16: But If Not

1. Gregg T. Johnson, *The Character of Leadership: Six Pillars of a Leader's Character* (Kearney: Morris Publishing, 2014), 70.

Day 18: Love Expressed

1. Matthew Henry, *Matthew Henry Commentary on the Whole Bible (Complete)*, Vol. 5, N.p., 1706, https://www.biblegateway.com/resources/matthew-henry/John.13.31-John.13.35.

Day 22: Hiding Place

1. Matthew Henry, *Matthew Henry Commentary on the Whole Bible (Complete)*, Vol. 3, N.p., 1706, https://www.biblegateway.com/resources/matthew-henry/ps.119.114.

Day 24: Let Your Soul Sing

1. Taken from entry for September 28 in *Streams in the Desert* (Kindle) by L.B. Cowman Copyright (c) 1996 by L.B. Cowman. Used by permission of Zondervan, www.zondervan.com.

Day 26: Undeserved Kindness

1. John Newton, "Amazing Grace," 1779, St. 5, A Collection of Sacred Ballads, 1790, public domain.

Day 35: Carry Your Cross

1. Matthew Henry, *Matthew Henry Commentary on the Whole Bible (Complete)*, Vol. 5, N.p., 1706, https://www.biblegateway.com/resources/matthew-henry/Matt.16.24-Matt.16.28.

Bibliography

Bloom, John. "But God." Desiring God. Accessed January15, 2021. https://www.desiringgod.org/articles/but-god.

Cowman, L.B. Streams in the Desert. Grand Rapids: Zondervan, 1996. Kindle.

Henry, Matthew. Matthew Henry Commentary on the Whole Bible (Complete). Vol. 3. N.p. 1706. https://www.biblegateway.com/resources/matthew-henry/ps.119.114.

Henry, Matthew. Matthew Henry Commentary on the Whole Bible (Complete). Vol. 5. N.p. 1706. https://www.biblegateway.com/resources/matthew-henry/John.13.31-John.13.35.

Henry, Matthew. Matthew Henry Commentary on the Whole Bible (Complete). Vol. 5. N.p. 1706. https://www.biblegateway.com/resources/matthew-henry/Matt.16.24-Matt.16.28.

Johnson, Gregg T. The Character of Leadership: Six Pillars of a Leader's Character. Kearney: Morris Publishing, 2014.

Newton, John. "Amazing Grace." 1779. St. 5. A Collection of Sacred Ballads, 1790. Public domain.

Spurgeon, Charles Haddon. "The Redeemer's Face Set Like a Flint." Metropolitan Tabernacle Pulpit, Vol. 47, November 28, 1880. Accessed January 15, 2021. https://www.spurgeon.org/resource-library/sermons/the-redeemers-face-set-like-a-flint/.

Thayer and Smith. "Greek Lexicon entry for Kardia." The NAS New Testament Greek Lexicon. Accessed January 15, 2021. https://www.biblestudytools.com/lexicons/greek/nas/kardia.html.

Order Information

To order additional copies of this book, please visit
www.thebluebirdpress.com
Also available on
Amazon.com and BarnesandNoble.com

www.ingramcontent.com/pod-product-compliance
Lightning Source LLC
Chambersburg PA
CBHW030450010526
44118CB00011B/868